Our Father

To my friends and family   G.N.

To Mary and Andrew   V.T.

Text by Mary Joslin
Illustrations copyright © 1999 Gail Newey
This edition copyright © 2003 Lion Publishing

The moral rights of the author and illustrator
have been asserted

Published by
Lion Publishing plc
Mayfield House, 256 Banbury Road,
Oxford OX2 7DH, England
www.lion-publishing.co.uk
ISBN 0 7459 4855 3

First hardback edition 1999
First paperback edition 2003
1 3 5 7 9 10 8 6 4 2 0

Acknowledgments
Bible extracts as follows taken from the Good News Bible: Psalms 19:1–4; 27:4; 130:1–4; Matthew
5:43–45; 6:24–27, 33. Scriptures quoted from the Good News Bible published by The Bible Societies/
HarperCollins Publishers Ltd, UK © American Bible Society 1966, 1971, 1976, 1992, 1994 used with
permission. Bible extracts as follows taken from the New Revised Standard Version: Psalms 23:1–4, 27:1,
13–14; 100:3–5; Luke 11:1–4 (some variant readings used); I Corinthians 13:4–8; Revelation 4:11;
21:1, 3–4. The Scripture quotations contained herein are from the New Revised Standard Version
of the Bible, Anglicized Edition, copyright © 1989, 1995 by the Division of Christian Education
of the National Council of the Churches of Christ in the United States of America, and are
used by permission. All rights reserved.

A catalogue record for this book is available
from the British Library

Typeset in 14/21 Berkeley Old Style BT
Printed and bound in Singapore

Our Father

The prayer Jesus taught

Meditations by Mary Joslin ❖ *Illustrations by Gail Newey*

LION
Children's Books

Introduction

The Our Father is the prayer that Jesus taught. Here is St Luke's account of what happened:

Jesus was praying in a certain place, and after he had finished, one of his disciples said to him, 'Lord, teach us to pray.' He said to them, 'When you pray, say:

Our Father in heaven, hallowed be your name.

Your kingdom come. Your will be done, on earth as in heaven.

Give us each day our daily bread.

And forgive us our sins, for we ourselves forgive everyone indebted to us.

And do not bring us to the time of trial, but rescue us from evil.'

Luke 11:1–4

In the centuries since that time, Christians all over the world have said Jesus' prayer in their own language. The version above is translated from the Bible itself. The translation used throughout this book is the one found in many prayer-books today.

Our Father

Sometimes,
when I am all alone,
I dream that I am not alone.

I dream that I am close
to One who loves me.

I see little children
safe in the arms of someone who loves them
and I dream of finding love like that,
strong and kind;
and I dream of finding love
that will keep me safe
for ever.

I have asked the Lord for one thing;
  one thing only do I want:
to live in the Lord's house all my life,
  to marvel there at his goodness,
  and to ask for his guidance.

Psalm 27:4

Who art in heaven

I look up at the skies
spreading wide to a great beyond,
an endless sea of stars and constellations.

Then I know for sure
there is more than I can see.

Then I wonder
what deep love
and powerful wisdom
holds the universe in place;
I wonder about the Greatness
that is above the universe
and beyond it.

How clearly the sky reveals God's glory!
How plainly it shows what he has done!
Each day announces it to the following day;
each night repeats it to the next.
No speech or words are used,
no sound is heard;
yet their message goes out to all the world
and is heard to the ends of the earth.

Psalm 19:1–4

Hallowed be thy name

Wonders are all around:
the fresh beauty of leaves;
the sparkling purity of splashing water;
the fierce majesty of the sun;
the gentle kindness of the warm breeze.

Such wonders whisper of the world's Great Maker
and call us to silence,
to reverence,
to worship.

'You are worthy, our Lord and God,
    to receive glory and honour and power,
for you created all things,
    and by your will they existed and
    were created.'

Revelation 4:11

Thy kingdom come

I am looking for an escape:
an escape from all that is grey and dreary.

I have glimpsed brightness just enough—
in flashes of beauty, in words of kindness—
and I am looking
for a world made new.

Then I saw a new heaven and a new earth;
for the first heaven and the first earth had
passed away, and the sea was no more.
And I heard a loud voice from the throne
saying, 'See, the home of God is among
mortals. He will dwell with them; they
will be his peoples, and God himself will
be with them; he will wipe every tear
from their eyes. Death will be no more;
mourning and crying and pain will be no
more, for the first things have passed away.'

Revelation 21:1, 3–4

Thy will be done on earth, as it is in heaven.

I am dreaming of the world
as it should be:
where there is laughter
and kindness,
generosity and love.

Jesus said,
'You have heard that it was said, "Love your friends, hate your enemies." But now I tell you: love your enemies and pray for those who persecute you, so that you may become the children of your Father in heaven. For he makes his sun to shine on bad and good people alike, and gives rain to those who do good and to those who do evil.'

Matthew 5:43–45

Give us this day our daily bread

All I need is
enough to sustain me
through life's great adventure,
travelling light,
travelling free,
travelling to the furthest shore.

Jesus said,
'No one can be a slave of two masters; he will hate one and love the other; he will be loyal to one and despise the other. You cannot serve both God and money.

   'This is why I tell you not to be worried about the food and drink you need in order to stay alive, or about clothes for your body. After all, isn't life worth more than food? And isn't the body worth more than clothes? Look at the birds: they do not sow seeds, gather a harvest and put it in barns; yet your Father in heaven takes care of them! Aren't you worth much more than birds? Can any of you live a bit longer by worrying about it?

   'Instead, be concerned above everything else with the Kingdom of God and with what he requires of you, and he will provide you with all these other things.'

Matthew 6:24–27, 33

And forgive us our trespasses

Each new day dawns
fresh and clean
and full of hope.

So many evenings end
with a sigh:
for foolishness that led to tears,
for mischief that turned to malice,
for the chances to do good
left neglected.

Then I long for these bad things
to be left behind
and forgotten.

From the depths of my despair
   I call to you, Lord.
Hear my cry, O Lord;
   listen to my call for help!
If you kept a record of our sins,
   who could escape being condemned?
But you forgive us,
   so that we should stand in awe of you.

Psalm 130:1–4

As we forgive those who trespass against us.

I do not want to be trapped
by the worst thing I ever did—
labelled and condemned.

I want the chance to learn,
to grow and to change.

For that reason, I shall give
the same chance to others.

Love is patient; love is kind; love is not envious
or boastful or arrogant or rude. It does not insist
on its own way; it is not irritable or resentful; it
does not rejoice in wrongdoing, but rejoices in
the truth. It bears all things, believes all things,
hopes all things, endures all things.
　　Love never ends.

1 Corinthians 13:4–8

And lead us not into temptation

Do not let my path
be too hard.

I do not want to find myself
in the midst of so much
wickedness and misery
that I give up believing
in goodness and love.

The Lord is my light and my salvation;
    whom shall I fear?
The Lord is the stronghold of my life;
    of whom shall I be afraid?

I believe that I shall see the goodness of the Lord
    in the land of the living.
Wait for the Lord;
    be strong, and let your heart take courage;
wait for the Lord!

Psalm 27:1, 13–14

But deliver us from evil.

*Keep me safe from the things that dishearten,
the things that terrify,
the things that destroy.*

The Lord is my shepherd, I shall not want.
   He makes me lie down in green pastures;
he leads me beside still waters;
   he restores my soul.
He leads me in right paths
   for his name's sake.

Even though I walk through the darkest valley,
   I fear no evil;
for you are with me;
   your rod and your staff—
   they comfort me.

Psalm 23:1–4

For thine is the kingdom, the power and the glory, for ever and ever. Amen.

In the early days of Christianity, the followers of Jesus added this ending to the prayer, expressing their confidence in God.

Know that the Lord is God.
It is he that made us, and we are his;
we are his people, and the sheep of his pasture.

Enter his gates with thanksgiving,
and his courts with praise.
Give thanks to him, bless his name.

For the Lord is good;
his steadfast love endures for ever,
and his faithfulness to all generations.

Psalm 100:3–5

Other titles from Lion Children's Books

The Story of the Cross   *Mary Joslin and Gail Newey*

Best-Loved Parables   *Lois Rock and Gail Newey*

The Lion Book of 1000 Prayers for Children   *Lois Rock*